All About Soil

Lamar Coldwell

Rosen REAL READERS

Rosen Classroom™
New York

1

Soil is important.
It helps plants grow.

It helps clean water.

Dirty water passes through.

It comes out clean.

Soil can be used to build.

Soil is a home for animals, too.

Prairie dogs live in the soil.

What other animals
live underground?

Words to Know

animal

plant

prairie dog

soil